D1293741

Amazing Elephants

Charlotte Guillain

Chicago, Illinois

© 2013 Raintree
an imprint of Capstone Global Library, LLC
Chicago, Illinois

Edited by Daniel Nunn, Rebecca Rissman, and Catherine Veitch
Designed by Victoria Allen
Picture research by Mica Brancic
Production by Victoria Fitzgerald
Originated by Capstone Global Library Ltd
Printed and bound in China by CTPS

17 16 15 14 13
10 9 8 7 6 5 4 3 2 1

Library of Congress Cataloging-in-Publication Data
Guillain, Charlotte.
  Amazing elephants / Charlotte Guillain.
    pages cm.—(Walk on the wild side)
  Includes bibliographical references and index.
  ISBN 978-1-4109-5216-5 (hb)—ISBN 978-1-4109-5223-3 (pb) 1. Elephants—Juvenile literature. I. Title.
  QL737.P98G85 2013
  599.67—dc23   2012034616

Acknowledgments
We would like to thank the following for permission to reproduce photographs:Alamy p. 15 (© Steve Bloom Images); Getty Images pp. 7 (National Geographic/Dr. John Michael Fay) 9 (Peter Arnold/Martin Harvey), 25 (Oxford Scientific/David Cayless); Nature Picture Library pp. 4 (© Andy Rouse), 8 (© Edwin Giesbers), 11 (© Tony Heald), 12 (© Jabruson), 14 (© Peter Blackwell), 17 (© Ben Osborne), 18 (© Karl Ammann), 20 (© Peter Blackwell), 21 (© Anup Shah), 23 (© Charlie Summers), 24 (© Lisa Hoffner), 26 (© Andy Rouse), 27 (© Anup Shah), 28 (© Vivek Menon), 29 (© Andy Rouse); Shutterstock pp. 5 (Rich Carey), 10 (Stephane Bidouze), 13 (© Cucumber Images), 16 (© Johan Swanepoel), 19 (Jonathan Pledger), 22 (© SouWest Photography).

Cover photograph of an elephant calf reproduced with permission of Shutterstock (© FWStupidio).

We would like to thank Michael Bright for his invaluable help in the preparation of this book.

Some words are shown in bold, **like this**. You can find out what they mean by looking in the glossary.

Contents

Introducing Elephants

The elephant is the largest animal living on land, but it is also very gentle and **intelligent**. There are three different **species** of elephant: Asian, African bush, and African forest elephants.

Asian elephants

African bush
elephants

Where Do Elephants Live?

Asian elephants live in India, Sri Lanka, and parts of Southeast Asia. African forest elephants live in **rain forests** in West and Central Africa. African bush elephants live on the **savannah** in many parts of Africa.

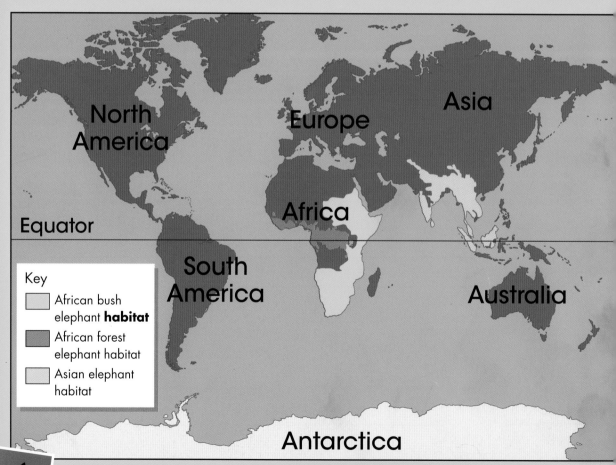

North America

Europe

Asia

Equator

Africa

South America

Australia

Key
African bush elephant **habitat**
African forest elephant habitat
Asian elephant habitat

Antarctica

African forest
elephant

What Do Elephants Look Like?

African bush elephants are the largest **species**. They can be up to 13 feet tall. That is over two times the height of an adult man. All elephants have thick, wrinkled, gray-brown skin that hangs in folds.

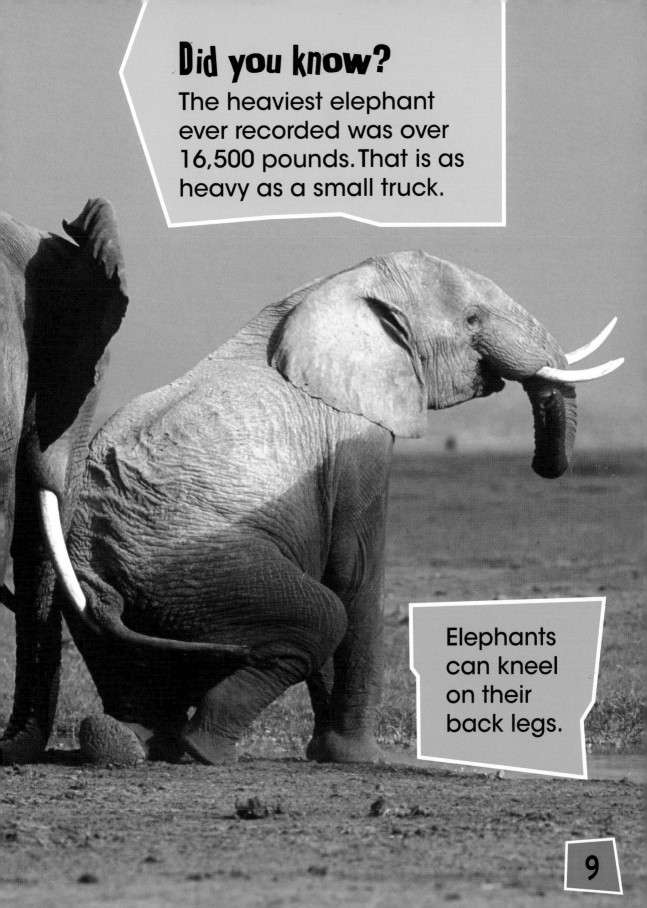

Did you know?
The heaviest elephant ever recorded was over 16,500 pounds. That is as heavy as a small truck.

Elephants can kneel on their back legs.

9

Enormous Ears

Elephants have huge ears. African bush elephants have much bigger ears than Asian elephants. African forest elephants have more rounded ears than bush elephants.

Asian elephant

Did you know?

African bush elephants can get very hot on the **savannah**. They flap their large ears to help them stay cool.

Trunk Power

Elephants can use their trunks to push or lift very heavy objects. But they can also grip and pick up tiny things. Elephants use their trunks to help them cool down. They suck water up their trunks and spray it over themselves.

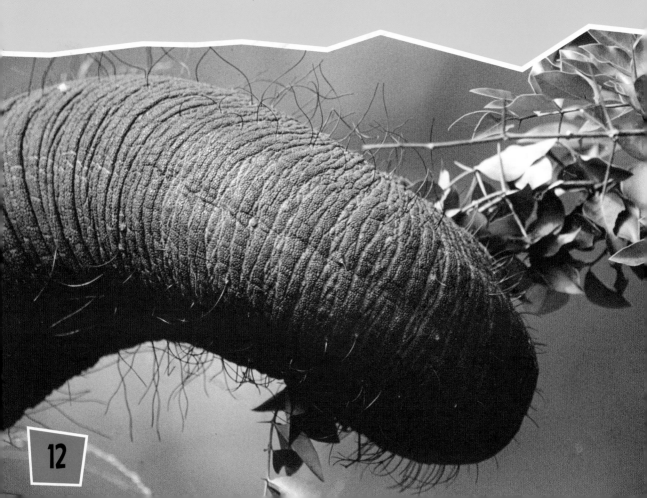

Asian elephant

Terrible Tusks

Most African elephants and some Asian elephants have tusks. Tusks are very long teeth that grow when the elephant loses its baby teeth. Elephants use their tusks to dig for food or strip bark off trees to eat.

African elephant

tusk

African
elephants

Male elephants sometimes use
their tusks to fight each other.

Eating and Drinking

Elephants eat grass, roots, leaves, bark, and fruit. These big animals need to eat huge amounts of food to get enough energy. They use their trunks to squirt water and put food into their mouths.

African elephant

Did you know?

Elephants can drink up to 40 gallons of water every day. Think of the size of a large milk jug and multiply it by 40!

African elephant

Life in a Herd

Elephants live in family groups called **herds**. Herds are made up of related female elephants and their babies. Adult male elephants leave the herd and either live alone or in small groups with other males.

There are usually around 10 elephants in a herd.

African elephants

African elephant

Male elephants
are called bulls.

Matriarchs

Female elephants are called cows. Each **herd** is led by an older cow called a **matriarch**. When a matriarch dies, the cow that is most closely related to her becomes the next matriarch.

African elephants

African elephants

The matriarch is very experienced and can show the rest of the herd where to find food and water.

Elephant Calves

Female elephants can be pregnant for 18 to 22 months. Mothers usually only have one baby at a time, called a calf. The **matriarch** teaches her daughters how to care for their calves.

Calves drink milk for around two years.

African elephants

All the elephants in the **herd** help to care for the calves.

African elephants

Keeping in Touch

Elephants in a **herd** are very good at **communicating**. They use their senses of sound, touch, and smell. Elephants can make a low rumbling sound that travels over a long distance to keep in touch with each other.

Elephants touch trunks to communicate.

African elephants

Did you know?
Elephants trumpet when they are scared or angry.

African bush elephant

Elephants Never Forget!

Elephants have very good memories. A **matriarch** can remember the way to a water hole that is many miles away, even if she has not been there for years.

African elephants

African
elephants

Did you know?

Older elephants pass
on their knowledge
to the younger
elephants in a **herd**,
so the herd can keep
the memory going.

Life for an Elephant

Sometimes humans hunt elephants for their tusks. Elephant **habitats** are also getting smaller. We need to protect this beautiful and amazing animal. Elephants are huge and can be dangerous. But people are still only starting to learn about how **intelligent** they are.

elephant tusk

Did you know?
Elephants can live for around 65 years.

African elephant

Glossary

communicate pass on and share information

habitat natural home for an animal or plant

herd group of elephants

intelligent smart

matriarch older female that leads a herd

rain forest area of forest with tall trees and a lot of rain

savannah area of grassland found in many parts of Africa south of the Sahara Desert

species type of animal

Find Out More

Books

Firestone, Mary. *Top 50 Reasons to Care About Elephants* (Top 50 Reasons to Care About Endangered Animals). Berkeley Heights, N.J.: Enslow, 2010.

Joubert, Beverly, and Dereck Joubert. *Face to Face with Elephants* (Face to Face with Animals). Washington, D.C.: National Geographic, 2008.

Thomas, Isabel. *Elephant vs. Rhinoceros* (Animals Head to Head). Chicago: Raintree, 2006.

Web sites

Facthound offers a safe, fun way to find web sites related to this book. All the sites on Facthound have been researched by our staff.

Here's all you do:
Visit **www.facthound.com**
Type in this code: 9781410952165

Index

ECHO PARK ELEMENTARY SCHOOL
ISD 196
14100 County Road 11
Burnsville, Minnesota 55337